D1282801

Sea Otters

by Nathan Sommer

BELLWETHER MEDIA • MINNEAPOLIS, MN

Note to Librarians, Teachers, and Parents:

Blastoff! Readers are carefully developed by literacy experts and combine standards-based content with developmentally appropriate text.

Level 1 provides the most support through repetition of high-frequency words, light text, predictable sentence patterns, and strong visual support.

Level 2 offers early readers a bit more challenge through varied simple sentences, increased text load, and less repetition of high-frequency words.

Level 3 advances early-fluent readers toward fluency through increased text and concept load, less reliance on visuals, longer sentences, and more literary language.

Level 4 builds reading stamina by providing more text per page, increased use of punctuation, greater variation in sentence patterns, and increasingly challenging vocabulary.

Level 5 encourages children to move from "learning to read" to "reading to learn" by providing even more text, varied writing styles, and less familiar topics.

Whichever book is right for your reader, Blastoff! Readers are the perfect books to build confidence and encourage a love of reading that will last a lifetime!

This edition first published in 2018 by Bellwether Media, Inc.

No part of this publication may be reproduced in whole or in part without written permission of the publisher. For information regarding permission, write to Bellwether Media, Inc., Attention: Permissions Department, 5357 Penn Avenue South, Minneapolis, MN 55419.

Library of Congress Cataloging-in-Publication Data

Names: Sommer, Nathan, author.
Title: Sea Otters / by Nathan Sommer.
Other titles: Blastoff! Readers. 3, Ocean Life Up Close.
Description: Minneapolis, MN : Bellwether Media, Inc., [2018] | Series: Blastoff! Readers: Ocean Life Up Close
  | Audience: Ages 5-8. | Audience: K to Grade 3. | Includes bibliographical references and index.
Identifiers: LCCN 2017028812 | ISBN 9781626177666 (hardcover : alk. paper) | ISBN 9781681034751 (ebook)
Subjects: LCSH: Sea otter–Juvenile literature.
Classification: LCC QL737.C25 S66 2018 | DDC 599.769/5–dc23
LC record available at https://lccn.loc.gov/2017028812

Editor: Paige V. Polinsky   Designer: Tamara JM Peterson

Printed in the United States of America, North Mankato, MN.

Table of Contents

What Are Sea Otters?

Sea otters are **mammals** with thick fur. They are the largest members of the **weasel** family.

badgers

stoats

wolverines

These animals are known
for floating on their backs.
They even sleep this way!

Sea otters are found near coasts along the Pacific Ocean. They like shallow, rocky waters best.

otter surrounded by kelp

life span:
up to 23 years

depth range:
0 to 148 feet
(0 to 45 meters)

sea otter range =

N
W E
S

conservation status: **endangered**

Extinct	Extinct in the Wild	Critically Endangered	Endangered	Vulnerable	Near Threatened	Least Concern

Sea otters often live around thick **kelp** forests. They hardly ever leave the water.

Sea otters are the smallest ocean mammals. They are usually about 4 feet (1.2 meters) long.

Sea Otter Size

4 feet (1.2 meters) long

average human

Most weigh between 40 and 65
pounds (18.1 and 29.5 kilograms).

Sea otters have thicker fur than any other animal. Their **double coats** help them stay warm in icy waters.

These thick coats are often dark brown. They keep sea otter skin completely dry!

Sea otters have round faces with long whiskers. Their ears and **nostrils** close underwater.

nostril

whiskers

Identify a Sea Otter

double coat

webbed feet

flat tail

These animals use flat tails and **webbed feet** to swim. Their back legs are longer than their front legs.

Shell Smashers

Sea otters hunt for food along the ocean floor. These **carnivores** can stay underwater for nearly six minutes!

They mostly eat **invertebrates** like clams, crabs, and squids. Small fish are also favorite meals.

Catch of the Day

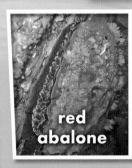
red abalone

purple sea urchins

market squid

crab

sea otter
smashing shell

Sea otters spend up to half
of their days hunting. But their
work does not end there.

Clams and crabs have tough shells. Sea otters use rocks as tools to smash these shells open and eat the meat inside.

clam

Raft Life

Sea otters live together in groups called **rafts**. This helps them stay safe from **predators** like sharks.

Sea otters usually stick together while they rest. Some even hold hands while sleeping!

Sea Enemies

great white sharks

orcas

California sea lions

sea otter raft

pup

Female sea otters
give birth to one **pup**
every year or two.

Before hunting, mothers tie their pups to kelp. It keeps the pups from floating away. The young otters will soon learn to hunt on their own!

kelp

Glossary

carnivores—animals that only eat meat

double coats—two layers of fur that protect sea otters from the cold waters they live in

invertebrates—animals without backbones

kelp—a type of large, brown seaweed

mammals—warm-blooded animals that have backbones and feed their young milk

nostrils—the two openings in a sea otter's nose that it breathes and smells through

predators—animals that hunt other animals for food

pup—a baby sea otter

rafts—groups of sea otters

weasel—any of a family of small, meat-eating animals that can hunt animals larger than themselves

webbed feet—feet with thin skin that connects the toes

To Learn More

AT THE LIBRARY

Jennings, Dorothy. *Otters Smash, Crabs Pinch*. New York, N.Y.: PowerKids Press, 2018.

Keogh, Josie. *What Are Sea Mammals?* New York, N.Y.: Britannica Educational Publishing in Association with Rosen Educational Services, 2017.

Rathburn, Betsy. *River Otters*. Minneapolis, Minn.: Bellwether Media, 2018.

ON THE WEB

Learning more about sea otters is as easy as 1, 2, 3.

1. Go to www.factsurfer.com.

2. Enter "sea otters" into the search box.

3. Click the "Surf" button and you will see a list of related web sites.

With factsurfer.com, finding more information is just a click away.

Index

The images in this book are reproduced through the courtesy of: Michael Gore/ FLPA, front cover; Magryt, p. 3 (sea otter); worldswildlifewonders, pp. 4-5, 21; Michal Ninger, p. 5 (bottom); Arto Hakola, pp. 5 (center), 9; charlie davidson, p. 5 (top); Kip Evans/ Alamy, p. 6; htrnr, p. 7; Chase Dekker, p. 20; Yulia_B, p. 10; theartist312, p. 11; Menno Schaefer, p. 12; Joe Morris 917, pp. 13 (bottom), 19; David Litman, p. 13 (top center); fred goldstein, pp. 13 (top left, top right), 18; David M G, p. 14; Jean-Edouard Rozey, pp. 15 (bottom); Southwest Fisheries Science Center/ NOAA Fisheries Service/ Wikipedia, p. 15 (top left); NatalieJean, p. 15 (top center); littlesam, p. 15 (top right); Tom & Pat Leeson/ age fotostock, p. 16; Kirsten Wahlquist, p. 17; Andrea Izzotti, p. 19 (top left, top center); Roger de Montfort, p. 19 (top right).

25·95